This book is dedicated to our clients.
Their resiliency and bravery inspire us every day.

www.jameonscloset.net

## A message to parents, teachers and clinicians

Jameon's Closet is a story written to help children acknowledge and respect their feelings...even the hard ones. It uses humor and everyday life to gently and non-threateningly expose children to the importance of appropriately expressing feelings. The clever use of the closet as a metaphor addresses a familiar and common experience many children have when confronted with overwhelming feelings. The authors invite children to engage in a process of cleaning as they go, little by little, which lends hope to an otherwise large goal. As children, and adults alike, embrace the important message of Jameon's Closet, we can expect maturity and well-being for all.

Ceth Ashen, Ph.D.
Clinical Psychologist

# JAMEON'S CLOSET

SHAUNA HAVLINA

M.S., LMFT

LEANNE RICHTER

M.A., LMFT

Jameon has a problem.

His grandma told him
to clean out his closet.

This wouldn't normally be a problem, but Jameon is scared to open the door.

For the last year, every time he had something he didn't want to look at anymore: an old magazine, a dirty sock, an empty juice box, he threw it in the closet.

It just felt like too much work to pick up that stinky piece of trash, walk **ALL THE WAY** to the garage, and throw it in the trash can.

At first it was no big deal. Grandma even let him play his game for an extra hour one day because his room looked so clean!

But really, his room wasn't clean at all. The mess just kept getting worse and worse. The pile grew bigger and bigger.

Until that closet looked like it was about to **BURST!**

Soon he couldn't fool grandma anymore. She started to smell something a little funny coming from under the door.

And then she realized Jameon didn't have any more socks.

So now he has to clean out the closet.
Or he can't play his game for a whole month.

And it just feels like too much work.

Luckily, Grandma knows someone who can help. Jon is a counselor.

He comes over to talk and he helps when things get rough.

Jon said it was going to be okay.

Jon had an idea...

Instead of bursting the door open and letting everything tumble out at once, they could take it little by little.

First they took a few socks and put them in the hamper.
Then, they found three juice boxes and put them in the trash.

Then they took a break and played a card game.
Jameon was starting to feel a little better. He could see
a ray of light coming out of the space in the closet!

It still took work, but Grandma said they could take
small steps and not feel so overwhelmed. With Grandma
and Jon's help, Jameon knew he could do it.

Soon the closet was neat and clean. He even found an old homework page that was worth 10 points at school!

Grandma was so proud!

Sometimes, feelings can get like Jameon's closet.

It's not easy to remember something bad that happened, or tell a friend about feeling sad.

So kids take ALL the memories and feelings and shove them in a closet. At first it's great! No bad feelings, no sad memories… but it doesn't last forever.
Soon something starts to smell a little funny.

Kids might start to act differently. Like getting mad and yelling at their friends. Or staying by themselves when they used to go outside and play.

The feelings closet is starting to get too full. But it doesn't have to burst.

Little by little, with the help of someone you trust, you can start to look at those old feelings and memories. Not too much at a time of course.

Little by little, the closet can get cleaned out.

# THE END

## About the Authors

Leanne and Shauna are licensed marriage and family therapists working with youth in Los Angeles County. They have spent the last ten years specializing in trauma related services for children and their families. Leanne now supervises clinicians working in the Juvenile Justice system and Shauna has a practice in Redding, CA.
For more information about the authors visits leannerichtermft.com and shaunahavlinatherapy.com.

www.ingramcontent.com/pod-product-compliance
Lightning Source LLC
Chambersburg PA
CBHW041558040426
42447CB00002B/213